A FUNNY, IRREVERENT SEDER SUF

TO CHANGE YOUR PASSOVER TRADITION FOREVER!

IT'S NOT B'SEDER!

זה לא בסדר!

by **Gary Swickley**

Dedicated to my wife, Pam, and our amazing children with whom we share our seder each year. They all enjoy a great sense of humor as well as tolerance for mine (even when it misses). Although our family drama went on all year round, it always reached a crescendo during our Passover seders.

It's Not B'Seder!

Cover and interior design by the Virtual Paintbrush.

ISBN (hardcover) 978-965-93169-1-5 • ISBN (paperback) 978-965-93169-0-8 • ISBN (ebook) 978-965-93169-2-2

First Edition March 2024

www.ItsNotBseder.com

TABLE OF CONTENTS

LIMERICKS

We are to enjoy our seder while leaning,
To add to our freedom's new meaning.
But it is no small act of labor,
Not to land on your neighbor,
Especially after a whole month of cleaning.

After hearing all the comments learned in classes,
The seder time so slowly passes.
Then the kids start to fight,
And we plow on despite,
But why drink only four glasses?

Why the big deal about dipping?
Is the story told really so gripping?
Dip the maror into charoses,
To see who could eat the mostest,
Not to mention all the stains from the dripping.

Moses refused to speak with his stutter,
To misrepresent words of G-d with each utter.
But with Aaron on his wing,
Moses managed to sing,
In the end, it was Pharaoh who would mutter.

6
3
1

There once was a man named Moses,
Whose grandfather, the king, made him brogez*.
Moses warned him to change,
And the Israel nation estrange,
Or he would make frogs come out of their noses.

* Hebrew slang for angry

Locusts, pestilence, boils, and lice,
Changing water to blood even twice.
Newborn babies are killed,
And desert bodies are grilled.
Chocolate cake - can I have another slice?

The seder has ritual traditions,
And we also have made some additions,
Like spilling wine on my pants,
And the off-color rants,
Not to mention a few seder omissions.

Just when you think that the seder is done,
Someone yells how about “Who Knows One?”.
While we may skip a few,
Or combine one or two,
Maybe next year we’ll do “Who Knows None?”!

At the seder we eat lots of horseradish,
And we cry even though we’re not saddish.
Then we laugh, eat, and sing,
And enjoy everything,
But yet, as it ends, we are gladdish.

My hunger pains are oh so strong,
We must have these rules all wrong.
No bread, pretzels, or rice,
A simple cracker would be nice.
Why is Pesach thirty-two days long!

At the seder, we eat like a pig,
Oh, these portions are really quite big.
Matzo needs to be a whole piece,
And maror's heat cannot cease,
Plus four glasses of wine in one swig!

Pharaoh chased all the Jews thru the sand,
Where it looked like he had them outmanned.
With the Jews' backs to the water,
The East Wind stopped their slaughter,
With the help of G-d's arm and strong hand.

Joseph sat in jail till he couldn't take her,
He saw the butler's release, not the baker.
When Pharaoh heard about the Jew,
Whose interpretations came true,
He made Joseph his kingdom's caretaker.

On Pesach, we eat the bread of affliction,
Of our slavery it provides a depiction.
As we are meant here to suffer,
We continue to stuff 'er,
'Til our bellies feel such great constriction.

Joseph was always quite proud,
Whose brothers threw him out of their crowd.
But when they all reunited,
Joe was so much delighted,
As per his dream, to him they all bowed!

Pharaoh had a dream that made no sense no how,
All explanations were just disavowed.
The skinny cows ate the fat,
But their bellies stayed flat,
Oh, I so wish that I was a cow!

All the miracles were really quite swell.
Blood, lice, frogs sure made us all kvell.
Finally, our G-d split the sea,
And we passed thru with glee,
Boy, I just can't wait for the sequel.

The wise and the one who can't ask,
The bad and simple – had their task,
With their own versions of why,
We must come up with a reply,
And on chag, without the help of a flask!

Constant affliction of our anguished nation
With non-stop pleas of our pain's cessation.
But no relief was in sight,
For our on-going plight,
Another year of Pesach constipation.

There once was a father named Jake,
Whose sons fought more than he could take.
But Joseph was proud,
And kept bragging out loud,
Until he was found in a pit with some snakes.

Swimming, eating out, whitewater roaring,
The beach, pool, and parasail soaring.
BBQs, rides on bikes,
And then rock climbing hikes,
Plus the constant whines that chag is so boring.

Every year we ask the same four questions,
But may I make some new suggestions?
Like how can one lean in a seat?
And how long till we eat?
And why eat till we reach indigestion?

The end of the seder, we race through,
Maybe skipping a section or two.
If I may be so rude,
To suggest adding some food,
Then the second half might be given its due.

Our slave saga each year is taught her,
Then to add we must taste salt water.
So to reminisce of our plight,
All our kids start to fight,
Next time, we'll just make the maror hotter.

Potiphar's wife found Joseph quite pretty,
To put him to work would be gritty.
She then made her play,
But he pushed her away,
Lo, the results for poor Joe were a pity.

GREEN EGGS AND CHAMETZ

(Inspired by Dr. Seuss's "Green Eggs and Ham")

Do you eat chametz on the chag?
I do not eat it, I just unplug.
I do not eat chametz on the chag.

I do not eat chametz on Passover,
Not until the chag is over.
I do not eat it with kneidel,
Even if it just touched the ladle.

I would not eat it at the seder,
I'm going to have to wait till later.
I won't eat chametz at the Kotel,
Not even at a five star hotel.

I won't eat it with the maror,
If I did, it would be a horror.
I won't eat it with the brisket.
You can try but I would not risk it.

If the flour even touched the yeast,
It could ruin the entire feast.
If the food had been fermented,
The afikoman prize would be relented.

I won't even eat the rice,
With the matzo, I must suffice.
I cannot even eat legumes,
Until the post-holiday period resumes.

I won't eat chametz with the wine,
Although the merlot is just divine.
I can't eat it with the karpas,
Although I don't get all the fuss.

Would you? Could you?
At the shul?
Eat it! Eat it!
Forget the rule!

I would not, could not
At the shul.

You may like it,
You don't know,
You may like it,
Forget the dough!

I would not, could not in a shul,
Not in a car! That won't be cool.
I cannot eat it in my sox,
I cannot eat it with my lox,
I cannot eat it at my table,
It's just not right, I'm just not able.
I cannot eat it here or there.
I cannot eat it anywhere.
I can't eat chametz all week long,
I cannot do it, it would just be wrong.

With chrain*! With chrain!
Could you, would you
Eat it with chrain?

Not with chrain! Not in a shul!
Not in a car! That won't be cool.
I would not, could not, in my sox,
I could not, would not, with my lox,
I could not eat it with my Rav,
I could not eat it with a glove.
I will not eat it here or there.
I will not eat it, I do not care.
I will not eat it, it won't be fair.

I won't eat it with charoset,
For all the dads would get upset.
Now all of these rules we must apply
Don't ask me, go ask your Rabbi!

* Chrain is Yiddish for horseradish

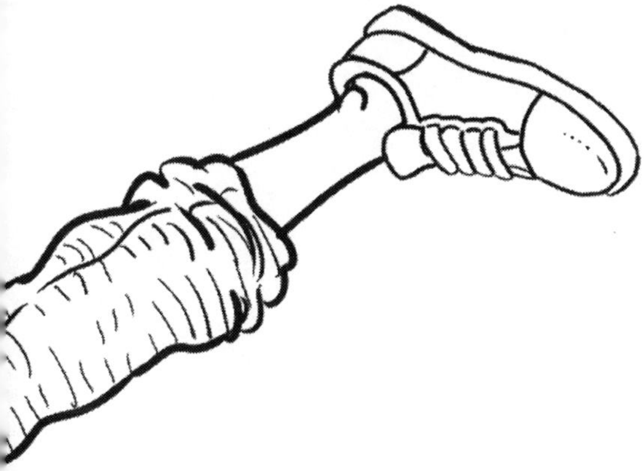

But after chag, I can go to town,
And eat the chametz upside down!
I will eat here and there,
I will eat it, I won't care.
I can eat it on the bus,
No one will even make a fuss.

But as to ham, that's another drama,
For that one, you better ask your Mama!

ONE COURSE TWO COURSE

(Inspired by Dr. Seuss's "One Fish Two Fish")

One course
Two course
Soup course
Of course.

Spicy dish
Hot knish
Full tish*
Gefilte fish.

This one your Mom just bought.
This one, in case, the first is not.
Say! What a lot of food we got.

* Yiddish term for table where guests gather around a table to eat and drink

Yes, some recipes are read.
And some just knew.
Some go cluck.
And some go moo.

Some guests are sad.
And some are mad.
And some are very, very bad.
Why are they sad and mad and bad?
From the way too much food they had!

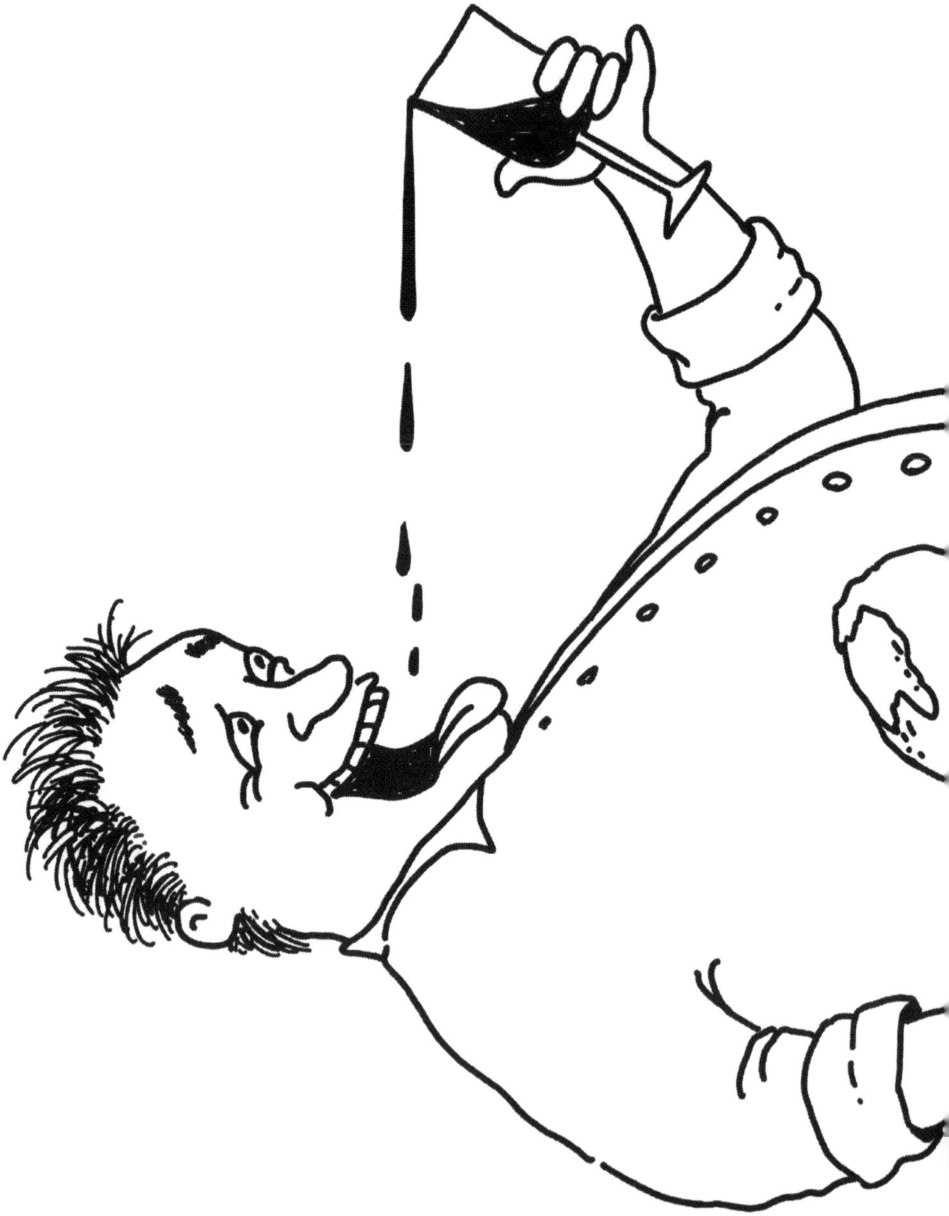

Some have high carbs. And some high fat.
Only the matzo will stay flat.
From there to here, from here to there,
Fattening things are everywhere!

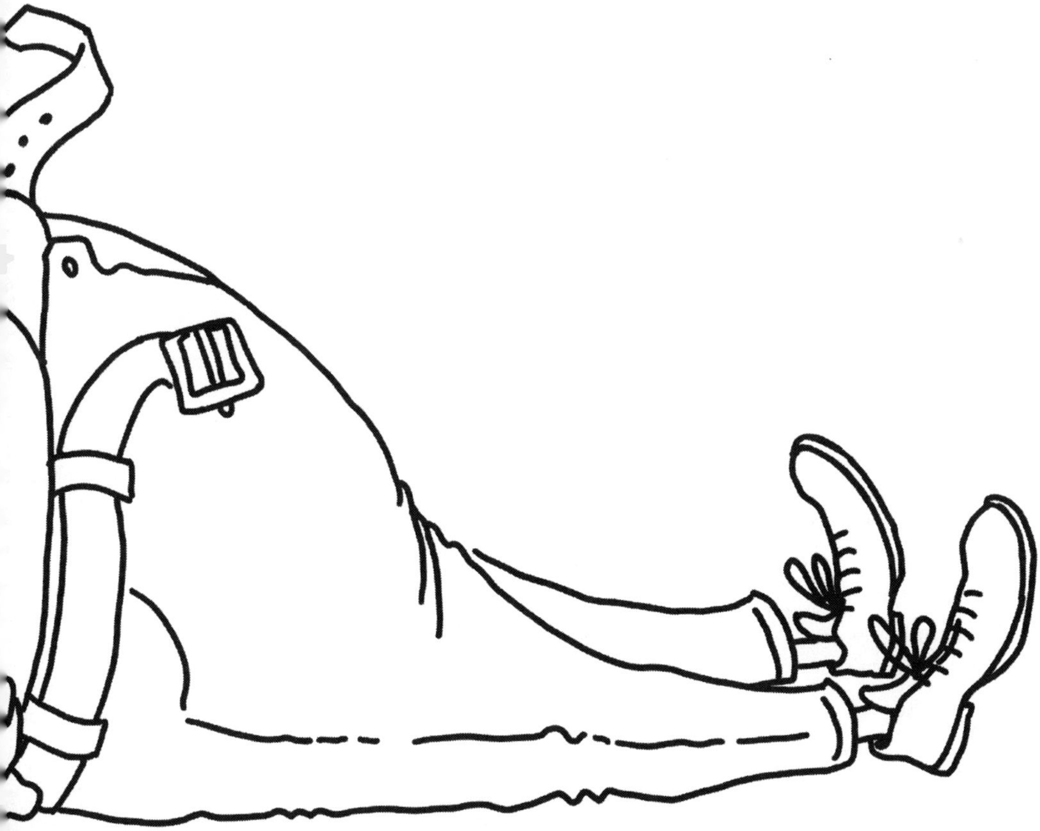

TOP TEN LISTS

Top Ten Expressions NEVER Heard at a Seder EVER

10 It’s my turn to wash the dishes.

9 I just wish Passover was a whole month long!

8 Can we sing each verse of Dayenu?

7 I got a party later tonight in Bnei Brak!

6 Only four glasses of wine?

5 I am so lucky that I am eighteen and still get to read the four questions.

4 It is only 1 a.m., can we sing some more songs?

3 Best part of living in *chul** is the second seder!

2 Leaning on pillows while we eat is so comfortable!

1 Why are we rushing through the seder so fast?

* Hebrew abbreviation for “Chutz La’aretz,” which means outside of Israel

Top Ten Ways Israel's Wizards were Greater than Egypt's Wizards

10 Could see Egyptian magician hide the ball up his sleeve

9 Non-Union

8 When Israelite wizard sawed Egyptian in half, they did not put him back together

7 Better finale

6 No cover charge

5 Better looking magicians' assistants

4 Could read Pharaoh's change of mind about releasing the children of Israel before Pharaoh could

3 Got little umbrellas with cocktails at Israelites' Vegas show

2 Israel's wizards' costumes had more bling

1 Aaron just had that X factor

Top Ten Reasons Why the Nation of Israel Wanted to Leave Egypt

10 Promised participation in FIFA World Cup

9 Fed up with the "Tastes Great, Less Filling" ads

8 Found leftover dead locusts everywhere

7 Continued to get mixed signals from Pharaoh

6 Guaranteed free cable for the first 40 years

5 Were pitched about new sure-fire weight loss manna diet

4 Beige color motif of Egypt was so played out

3 Offered free Bon Jovi tickets

2 Tired of going to see the Pyramids every year for vacation

1 Kept losing the ping pong balls in the slaves' rec room due to desert windstorms

Top Ten Plagues Not Mentioned in the Bible

10 "The Crown" was cancelled from Egyptian Netflix Service

9 Became NY Met fans

8 Kept getting lost in sandstorms on the way home from bingo each Tuesday night

7 Heartburn from the cholent every week

6 Could not get the sand out of their shoes

5 Israeli slave women constantly whining about humidity

4 Ran out of salsa way before tortillas were finished

3 Justin Bieber songs blasted from the heavens all over Egypt

2 Kept raising the Amazon Prime fee every two months

1 Daily wedgies of all Egyptian men

SEDER NIGHTS

(Sung to the tune of "Summer Nights"
from the soundtrack of "Grease")

Pesach seders started so long ago,
When G-d brought it to the cruel king Pharaoh.
Moses started with his lisp and his pleas,
Till Pharaoh was begging us to leave!
Chol Hamoed days just chilling away,
But oh, oh, those seder nights.

Uh, well-a, well-a, well-a, huh!

Tell me more, tell me more,
Like did you have to cook?
Tell me more, tell me more,
Afikoman, did you look?

Uh-huh, uh-huh, uh-huh, uh-huh!

The Jews all cried until G-d heard their plea,
He brought in Moses to set them all free.
Sent in blood, frogs, and even some lice,
Pharaoh soon learned that power came with a price.
First born son, something's begun,
But oh, oh, those seder nights.

Uh, well-a, well-a, well-a, huh!

ELL ME MORE!
TELL ME MORE!

Tell me more, tell me more,
Did the maror have bite?
Tell me more, tell me more,
Did the kids start to fight?

Uh-huh, uh-huh, uh-huh, uh-huh!

Locust, disease, then there was hail,
Pharaoh's resistance continued to fail.
Egyptians chased us when we started to flee,
But got washed out when they got to the sea.
All the warnings, don't mean a thing,
But oh, oh, those seder nights.

Whoa, whoa, whoa!

Tell me more, tell me more,
Were all the questions a bore?
Tell me more, tell me more,
Just know the answer is four!

Shoo-bop bop, shoo-bop bop,
shoo-bop bop, shoo-bop bop
Shoo-bop bop, shoo-bop bop,
shoo-bop bop, yeah!

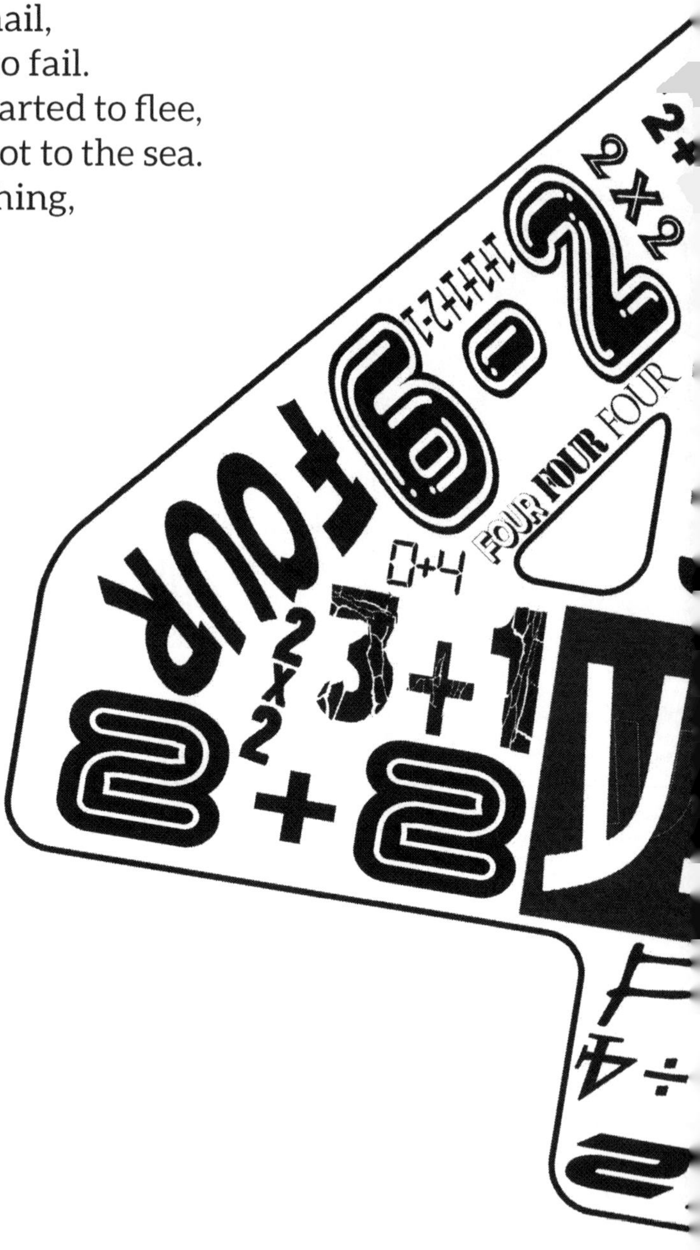

We were freed but that's not how it ends,
We then got the Torah, and killed our weekends!
We should know that it was all in his plan,
Just to bring us back to our land.
Endless cleaning, looking for meaning,
But oh, oh, those seder nights.

Whoa, whoa, whoa!

Tell me more, tell me more,
*Chumras** you can't ignore,
Tell me more, tell me more,
I heard they wash down the doors!

With all the new laws, there is no end,
Just like the money that we need to spend.
With family and friends we get to be,
But without the sand from the Red Sea.
Pesach struggles somehow all come out right,
But oh, those seder nights.

Tell me more, tell me more...

* Hebrew for religious law stringencies

SHOULD WE
SHOULD WE

SHOULD WE STAY OR SHOULD WE GO?

(Sung to the tune of the Clash's "Should I Stay or Should I Go?")

Pharaoh, you got to let me know,
Should we stay or should we go?
If you let us serve our Lord,
G-d will spare you from his sword,
So you got to let us know,
Should we stay or should we go?

It's always work, work, work,
But G-d will remove your smirk,
One day is bad and the next is worse,
And soon you will live the curse,
Well, your troubles will only grow -
So should we stay or should we go?

Should we stay or should we go now?
Should we stay or should we go now?
If we go, the sea will be trouble,
And if we stay, it will be double!
So come on Pharaoh let us know!

Your hesitation's bugging me,
Just back off and set us free,
With whom you are trying to mess,
Free us now and suffer less,
Come on and let us know,
Should we drey or should we blow?

Should we stay or should we go now?
Should we stay or should we go now?
If we go, there will be trouble,
And if we stay, it will be double!
So come on Pharaoh let us know,
Should we duel or should we blow?
Should we stay or should we go?
If we go, the sea will be trouble,
And if we stay, it will be double!
So you got to let us know,
Should we stay or should we go?

RIDDLES

Three answers are provided and the riddle challenge is to figure out the three questions (think Jeopardy). To make it more fun, the three questions rhyme! We suggest to give hints for the easiest of the three questions and then the others will become very guessable, but still challenging. This is a great group activity for all ages.

The Answer is: A Baby Goat, a British Pound, and Moses.

The Resolving Question is: What are a Kid, a Quid, and a Yid?

A: One of the Four Sons, Moses Gave Ten to Pharaoh, and Pharaoh's Agreement to Allow Us to Leave Egypt.

Q: What are Wise, Tries, and Lies?

A: We Do This Twice Before We Eat, Veggie Not on the Seder Plate, and Mo's Successor.

Q: What are Wash, a Squash, and Josh?

A: Moses' Arms During the War, Plague of Darkness, and a Result of Grating Horseradish.

Q: What are Weary, Eerie, and Teary?

A: One of the Plagues, Number of Dips, and Kitniyot.

Q: What are Lice, Twice, and Rice?

A: A Traditional Seder Food Item, Afikoman Negotiating Technique, and a Shank Bone.

Q: What are an Egg, Beg, and a Leg?

A: Our Seder's Salsa, Gaza's Area, and Tool Used to Strike Jewish Slaves.

Q: What are a Dip, a Strip, and a Whip?

A: How to Sit at the Seder, Pharaoh's Wife, and How We Prepare for Pesach.

Q: What are Lean, Queen, and Clean?

A: One of the Plagues, ADHD Slaves' Deficiency, and Pharaoh's Wizards Magic.

Q: What are Locusts, Focus, and Hocus Pocus?

A: The Haggadah, Lavan, and HaCarmel.

Q: What are a Book, a Crook, and a Shuk?

A: The Story of Our Exodus, Prelude to the Festive Meal, and the Matzo Effect.

Q: What are Emancipation, Anticipation, and Constipation?

A: We Must Drink Four of These, Where the Manna Came From, and a Great Afikomen Present.

Q: What are a Cup, Up, and a Pup?

A: A Latter Plague, Leah's Prop, and Joseph's Punishment.

Q: What are Hail, a Veil, and Jail?

A: The Number of Patriarchs, Pharaoh Ignored This From Moses, and Egypt's Waterloo.

Q: What are Three, a Plea, and Red Sea?

A: The Number of Cups of Wine,
Passover Cleaning, and a Long Seder.

Q: What are Four, More, and a Bore?

A: One of the Four Questions, Our Constant Search Goal, and a Side Effect of the Frog Plague.

Q: What are Leaning, Meaning, and Greening?

A: Joseph's Landing Spot, Precursor to Leaning, and a Red Sea Trick.

Q: What are a Pit, a Sit, and a Split?

A: The Jews Did This to the Lambs, Puah Did Not Have to Save This, and This May Be Salty at the Seder.

Q: What are Slaughter, a Daughter, and Water?

A: Four Challenges, Pesach No-No, and Number of Frogs During the Plague.

Q: What are Sons, Buns, and Tons?

A: Moses' Grandfather, Passover's Season, and an Expensive Afikoman Present.

Q: What are King, Spring, and Bling?

WHO KNOWS ONE?

Who Knows One?
One is the number of days of counting the Omer until you usually mess up the count.

Who Knows Two?
Two is the number of minutes until the youngest child at the seder complains that they are bored.

Who Knows Three?
Three is the number of people still left awake at the table at the end of the seder.

Who Knows Four?
Four is number of tries that it took Moses to utter the snake trick due to his stutter.

Who Knows Five?
Five is the number of times that Aunt Rose will mention that matzo gives her constipation.

Who Knows Six?
Six is the real number of the "four sons" if you include Irving and Sam.

Who Knows Seven?
Seven is the number of times that Pharaoh responded "No Way" to Moses' plague predictions.

Who Knows Eight?
Eight is the number of seconds until the kids give up on finding the afikoman and go with the whining technique instead.

Who Knows Nine?
Nine is the number of times that the father will threaten to make the seder go on until 2 in the morning if the kids don't shut up.

Who Knows Ten?
Ten is the number of Egyptian pounds wagered in the bet between Aaron and Pharaoh's magicians on the blood trick.

Who Knows Eleven?
Eleven is the number of times the chosen reader does not know the place in the Haggadah for their reading rotation.

Who Knows Twelve?
Twelve is the number of "I told you so"s that Joseph told his brothers at the "Big Reveal" in Egypt.

Who Knows Thirteen?
Thirteen is the number of hours it feels like until we can eat already!

Who Knows Fourteen? (For you really zealous participants!)
Fourteen is the number of times that your wife will say that next year she will not eat so much at the seder.

A BETTER PLAN

Although G-d made Egypt pay quite the price,
With the plagues of blood and then some lice.
He gave them wild beasts and horrible disease,
But he could have done much worse than these.
Although he caused much trepidation
To the entire Egyptian nation,
G-d's plan successfully ran its course,
But I think I could have made it worse.

Although G-d did not ask me any questions,
I did come up with a great suggestion.
Darkness was a good one and, of course, there was hail.
But compared to my idea, these plagues would just pale.
I think frogs would be considered child's play,
Compared to the evil I would display!

See, I would have created a horseradishasaurus,
Whose maror strength would be the worstest.
It would consume all eaters with great fear,
And make every eye fill up with tears.
The plague of boils would be like roses,
Compared to the fire coming out of their noses!

Oh, I am not even close to done;
In fact, I'm only starting to have fun.
I would make them eat oh so much food,
Soup, kugel, brisket that was stewed,
Gefilte fish, coleslaw, and then dessert.
Their buttons would be popping off their shirts.
Their stomachs would be aching in such pain,
And just when they started to complain,
I'd give them more ice cream on their pie.
Just for fun, I don't know why!

I would make them eat matzo in such a big portion,
Their faces and bellies would ache in contortion.
I would clog them all up with constipation.
These Egyptians would learn not to start up with OUR nation.
G-d let them off easy as he is truly kind,
But for me, I got a better plan in mind.

PASSOVER SPELL

We all know the bread of affliction
And its crunchy, messy tone.
It's one of our favorite seder topics,
But one thing is still unknown.

Is that matzo with an "o" or "a" or "h",
Should it be capitalized or not?
These questions can turn a scholar's head,
So we really don't have a shot.

But this is nothing compared to the conundrum
Of the one that lays ahead.
Is it Chanukah or Hanukkah
Or Hanukah instead??

Matzo noun

Mat•zo (mat-sə) **also** -(ˌ)sō

Variants *or* matzoh *or* matzah *or* matza *or* Matzo *or* Matzoh *or* Matzah *or* Matza

1 : unleavened bread eaten especially at the Passover
2 : a wafer of matzo

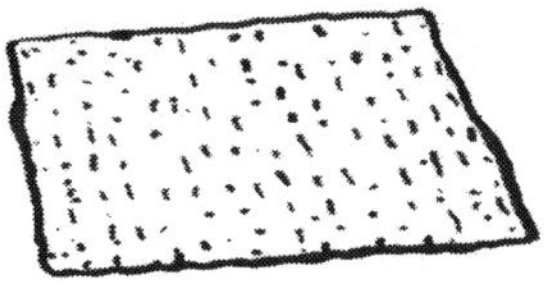

3 : controversial traditional Passover bread with a few thousand years of a love/hate relationship with the Jewish people

STILL LOOKING

I've sailed the Atlantic and Pacific Oceans,
And from sea to shining sea.
I looked in lakes from coast to coast,
From Alaska to the Florida Keys.

I've seen lots of tuna, herring, bass,
Pike, swordfish, and even cod.
Trout, goldfish, mackerel, and whale,
But one thing is very odd.

Despite my search from far to near,
In pursuit of my endless wish,
The one sea creature that I have never seen
Is the yummy gefilte fish!

ACKNOWLEDGEMENTS

While all of the textual content herein is totally my own, I want to shout out to some of the great muses that inspired much of this work. First of all, Shel Silverstein, a literary and graphic genius, who always left me feeling "that was so clever, I wish I had thought of that!" Also much appreciation to Dr. Seuss (he so should be Jewish; after all, he was a "doctor"!) and the Clash. I am sure this was the first time in history that those two artists were ever mentioned in the same sentence. "Summer Nights" from Grease has been seared into my brain by my children's endless viewing of this classic musical in their youth. Further, thanks to David Letterman for his legendary Top Ten Lists and Johnny Carson with his Carnac the Magnificent segment. I think they are both really Jewish as well.

The graphics were all my ideas brought to reality by an incredibly talented graphic artist, Ricky Castillo via Fiverr. Also thanks to Devorah Ohayan, a staff member of mine at Kosher Casual, who helped and always takes our graphics to the next level with her creativity. Shanie Cooper was the book layout graphic artist who professionally created this challenging book layout with care and patience.

Made in United States
Orlando, FL
08 April 2024

45584909R00037